D0852338

DEREK
JETER

DEREK
JETER

CARL EMERSON
THE CHILD'S WORLD®, INC.

ON THE COVER...

Front cover: Derek rounds the bases during a 1998 game.
Page 2: Derek smiles during practice at Atlanta's Turner Field on October 22, 1999.

Published in the United States of America by The Child's World®, Inc.
PO Box 326
Chanhassen, MN 55317-0326
800-599-READ
www.childsworld.com

Product Manager Mary Berendes
Editor Katherine Stevenson
Designer Mary Berendes

Photo Credits
© AFP/CORBIS: 6, 13, 16, 20
© AP/WideWorld Photos: 9, 10, 19, 22
© Reuters NewMedia Inc./CORBIS: 2, 15
© Rob Tringali Jr./SportsChrome-USA: cover

Library of Congress Cataloging-in-Publication Data
Emerson, Carl.
Derek Jeter / by Carl Emerson.
p. cm.
Includes index.
ISBN 1-56766-971-9 (alk. paper)
1. Jeter, Derek, 1974–   .—Juvenile literature.
2. Baseball players—United States—Biography—Juvenile literature.
[1. Jeter, Derek, 1974– 2. Baseball players. 3. Racially mixed people—Biography.]
I. Title.
GV865.J48 E44 2000
796.357'092—dc21

00-012257

TABLE OF CONTENTS

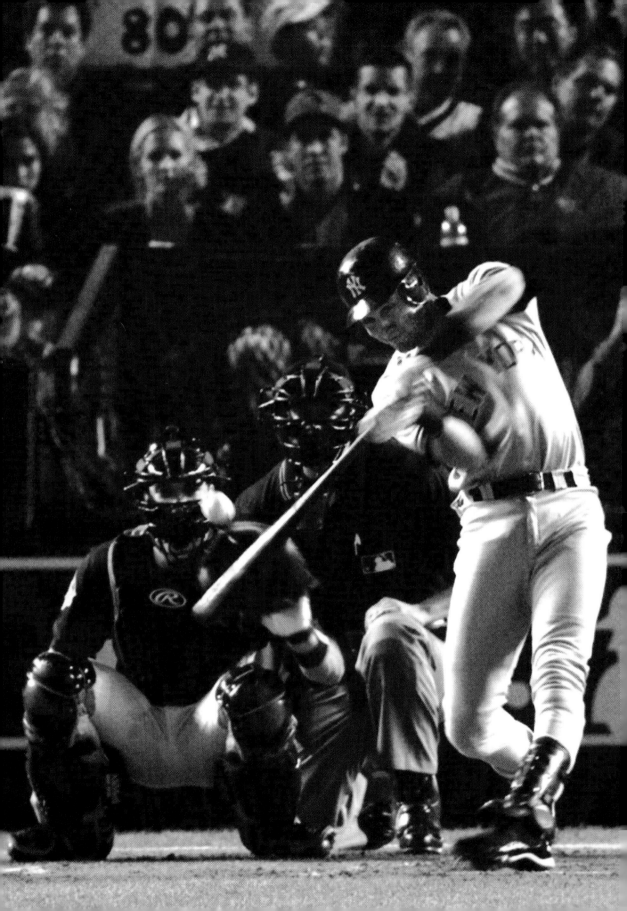

CLUTCH PLAYER

The New York Yankees were in an unfamiliar position. Playing in the 2000 World Series against the New York Mets, their rivals from across town, the Yankees had lost a game. In each of the previous two seasons, the Yankees had won the World Series in four straight games. This time, they had lost the previous night's game and were leading the Mets only two games to one.

In a surprise move, Yankees manager Joe Torre put Derek Jeter first in the **batting order**. Derek usually bats second or third for the Yankees. The Mets' Bobby Jones wound up and delivered the first pitch of the game, and Derek hit it over the left-field fence for a **home run**. The Yankees were on their way to another win.

If they could defeat the Mets the next night, the Yankees would win another World Series championship. The Mets were ahead 2–1 going into the sixth inning. With one out, Derek stepped to the plate and hit another home run, this time against pitcher Al Leiter. Derek's homer tied the game, and the Yankees went on to win the game—and the World Series. Derek Jeter was named the Series' Most Valuable Player.

← Derek hits a home run on the opening pitch
of game 4 of the 2000 World Series.

BIG DREAMS

Derek Jeter was born to be a New York Yankee. He was born on July 26, 1974, in Pequannock, New Jersey. His mother, Dorothy, had 13 brothers and sisters, so Derek had many aunts and uncles. Most of them were Yankees fans, and it didn't take long for Derek to become one, too.

When he was five, Derek and his family moved to Kalamazoo, Michigan. But that didn't change Derek's love for the Yankees. In fact, every summer he would go back to New Jersey to visit family, and they would go to games at New York's Yankee Stadium. He dreamed that someday he would be able to play for the Yankees in that stadium.

Lots of kids dream about playing **professional** sports. Derek was willing to put in the work it takes to actually get there. His father, Charles, encouraged him to play baseball. But Charles and Dorothy knew there was more to life than sports. They made sure Derek worked hard at all aspects of his life—his schoolwork, his family life, his friendships—as well as sports. In fact, they wouldn't let Derek play baseball unless his grades were good.

Derek throws the ball during batting practice before game 2 of the 2000 American League division series.

GROWING INTO HIS POSITION

Derek always wanted to play shortstop, one of the most important positions in baseball. A shortstop has to be quick and smart. A shortstop also has to have good hands and a strong, accurate throw. Derek had all of those qualities and more.

When Derek was growing up in Kalamazoo, Charles often coached Derek's teams. Charles could have made Derek the shortstop right away, but he wanted Derek to prove he was ready for such an important position. So Charles put Derek at second base. He taught Derek that it would take hard work to be a top baseball player. He wouldn't let him get away with complaining to coaches or umpires. He taught him to worry only about the things he could control himself.

When Derek was in ninth grade, he started out on the **junior varsity** team at Kalamazoo Central High School. The starting varsity shortstop was a top player, so Derek would have to wait his turn. It soon became clear to the coaches, however, that Derek was good enough to play on the varsity team. Near the end of the season, the varsity shortstop agreed to switch to third base so Derek could play shortstop.

← Pittsburgh Pirate Pat Meares (2) flies through the air toward Derek in an attempt to break up a first-inning double play on March 4, 2000.

HIGH SCHOOL WONDER

In high school, Derek became one of the top players in Michigan. By his senior year, he was one of the one of the best in the country. The nation's top colleges all wanted him to come play for their teams. However, many professional teams were now sending scouts to watch Derek play. Derek didn't let the scouts down. The American Baseball Coaches Association named him the 1992 High School Player of the Year. He also won the Gatorade High School Player of the Year Award for baseball.

Derek and his parents knew that he was going to get **drafted** by a professional team at the end of his senior season. They also knew he was going to have a tough decision to make—to sign a **contract** to play professional baseball or to go to college. Derek was prepared to go to the University of Michigan. As the draft day drew closer, he thought he would get drafted by the Cincinnati Reds. On June 1, 1992, the day of the draft, the phone rang in the Jeter home. Dorothy answered. It was the Yankees calling to say they that they had chosen Derek in the sixth pick of the draft. Derek's dreams were starting to come true!

Derek's parents knew he wanted to sign with the Yankees, but they also wanted him to go to college. Derek knew that if he signed with the Yankees, he could still take college courses during the off-season. When the Yankees offered to pay for Derek's college in addition to his salary, Derek signed his contract. So far, Derek has taken several courses at the University of Michigan.

Derek slides across home plate to score the winning run in a game against the Texas Rangers on April 27, 2000.

MOVING AWAY

Most players who are drafted by a professional baseball team start out in the **minor leagues.** The levels of play in the minor leagues are not as good as in the **major leagues,** where the Yankees play. There are several minor-league levels—**rookie league,** Class A, Class AA, and Class AAA. Most minor-league players never make it to the major leagues. Those who do need several years to work their way up to the majors.

Derek started out with the Yankees' rookie league team in Florida. He was miserable, because he had never lived away from home before. His play on the field got worse because he was so unhappy. He was only 18 years old, and he was far from home. Over time, however, Derek proved how strong he was. With the help of his coaches, he began to feel more comfortable, both on and off the field. He was ready to become a star again.

RISING STAR

In 1994, Derek started the season with the Yankees' Class A team in the Florida State League. He was outstanding, batting .329 and stealing 28 bases. In June, the Yankees moved him up to Class AA, and he got even better. He batted .377 there, and the Yankees moved him up to their Class AAA team in Columbus, Ohio. Again, he was great, batting .349 and playing well in the field.

Derek leaps high to make a catch as the Atlanta Braves' Andruw Jones slides in safely on June 2, 2000.

Derek's rise through the minor leagues was amazing. Few players are able to jump up so many levels so quickly. Now, Derek was only one level from the major leagues—and from his chance to play with the Yankees! At the end of 1994, *The Sporting News* named Derek the Minor League Player of the Year.

THE BIG JUMP

New York is the biggest city in the U.S., and the Yankees have lots of fans all around the country. People were getting excited to see Derek play for the team. But at the start of the 1995 season, the Yankees still had a **veteran** player, Tony Fernandez, at shortstop. So, Derek started the season in Class AAA at Columbus.

In May, the Yankees were not playing very well, and Fernandez was hurt. Instead of using a backup player from the major leagues, the Yankees brought Derek up from Columbus. It was a surprise, because many people thought the Yankees would leave Derek in the minors all season.

Derek made his major-league start on May 29 in the Seattle Kingdome. He didn't get any hits, but he played well in the field. At just 20 years old, Derek was the youngest player in the American League and the second youngest ever to play for the Yankees. The next night, Derek got two hits. On June 2, he realized his biggest dream, playing for the Yankees in Yankee Stadium.

Derek poses for photographers as he holds the MVP Trophy for the All-Star Game on July 11, 2000.

Derek stayed with the Yankees for a couple of weeks. Once Fernandez was ready to play again, the Yankees sent Derek back to Columbus so he could keep playing instead of sitting on the bench. When the minor-league season ended in September, Derek came back up to the Yankees and finished the season with them. In his 15 games with the Yankees, he batted .250—below his usual standards—but it was a valuable experience. He was getting ready to be a full-time big-leaguer.

A MAGICAL SEASON

In 1996, Derek started the season with the Yankees. "This is something I've been waiting for my entire life," he said. "I love New York." Once the Yankees made him their full-time shortstop, Derek was determined to prove that he belonged. And he was going to make sure he stayed in the major leagues.

In his first season, Derek did all of that and more. He batted .314 and had 78 runs batted in. He was named the American League Rookie of the Year, and he helped the Yankees win the World Series. Not only was he a star on his favorite team since childhood, he was a champion!

Derek hits a solo home run during the sixth inning of game 5 of the 2000 World Series.

→

NEW YORK, NEW YORK

Each year, Derek has become a better player. He is now regarded as one of the best players in all of baseball. In 1998, his third year with the Yankees, Derek batted .324, had 84 RBIs, and stole 30 bases. He also hit 19 home runs, the most ever by a Yankees shortstop. In the field, he made only 9 errors. The Yankees again won the World Series.

In 1999, Derek batted .349, the best average of his career so far. He also had 102 RBIs and broke his own record for homers by a Yankees shortstop, hitting 24. Again, the Yankees were World Series champions. In 2000, Derek had another great year, batting .339, and the Yankees won their third straight championship. He also was Most Valuable Player of both the All-Star Game and the World Series.

A BRIGHT FUTURE

Many great players go their entire careers without winning a championship. Derek has won four championships in five years, and he's only 26 years old! Derek has a long career ahead of him. Many people believe that he is already one of the best shortstops in the history of the game. Only time will tell if that's true. Right now, however, it looks as though Derek Jeter is headed for the Hall of Fame.

In game 5 of the 2000 World Series, Derek and his teammates celebrate after the go-ahead run scores in the ninth inning.

TIMELINE

July 26, 1974	Derek Sanderson Jeter is born in Pequannock, New Jersey.
1979	The Jeter family moves to Kalamazoo, Michigan.
1989	As a freshman, Derek makes the varsity team at Kalamazoo Central High School.
1992	Derek is named High School Player of the Year and wins the Gatorade High School Player of the Year Award.
June 1, 1992	The New York Yankees choose Derek in the sixth pick of the draft, and he reports to the Yankees' rookie league team in Florida.
1994	After climbing from Class A to Class AAA, Derek is named Minor League Player of the Year by *The Sporting News.*
May 29, 1995	Derek makes his major-league debut with the Yankees at the Seattle Kingdome.
June 2, 1995	Derek plays his first game in Yankee Stadium.
1996	In his first year as a full-time major-leaguer, Derek wins the American League Rookie of the Year award, and the Yankees win the World Series.
1998	Derek breaks the Yankees' record for home runs by a shortstop with 19, and the Yankees win the World Series.
1999	Derek snaps his own record by hitting 24 homers, and the Yankees repeat as World Series champions.
2000	Derek wins the Most Valuable Player award at the All-Star Game. The Yankees again win the World Series, and Derek is named Most Valuable Player of the Series.

Derek poses for photographers before the *Sports Illustrated* Sportsman of the Year awards on December 12, 2000.

GLOSSARY

batting order (BAT-ting OR-der)
The batting order is the list of players that shows when they will get to bat in a baseball game. Derek Jeter usually is listed second or third in the Yankees' batting order.

contract (KON-trakt)
A contract is the agreement an athlete signs when he or she is hired by a team. Derek Jeter signed a contract to play for the New York Yankees.

drafted (DRAF-ted)
When teams in a professional sports league choose new players for their teams, the players are drafted. The New York Yankees selected Derek Jeter with the sixth pick in the 1992 draft.

home run (HOME RUN)
A home run is a hit that lets the batter run around all the bases and back to home plate, scoring a run. Derek Jeter holds the Yankees record for home runs hit by a shortstop.

junior varsity (JOON-yer VAHR-sih-tee)
In high school and college sports, varsity is the top level of play, and junior varsity is the second-best level.

major leagues (MAY-jor LEEGZ)
The major leagues are the highest level of professional baseball. Derek Jeter made it to the major leagues in 1995.

minor leagues (MY-nor LEEGZ)
The lower levels of professional baseball are called the minor leagues. Derek Jeter started out in the minor leagues after he was drafted by the Yankees.

professional (pro-FESH-uh-nul)
In sports, a professional is someone who is good enough to be paid rather than just playing for fun. Derek Jeter is a professional baseball player.

rookie (ROOK-ee)
In professional sports, players in their first year are called rookies. Derek Jeter had an outstanding rookie year.

veteran (VET-er-un)
In sports, a veteran is a player who has been playing for quite a while. Derek Jeter is now a veteran player.

INDEX